SCIENCE WIDE OPEN
Women in Medicine

Written by Mary Wissinger
Illustrated by Danielle Pioli

Science, Naturally!
An imprint of Platypus Media, LLC
Washington, D.C.

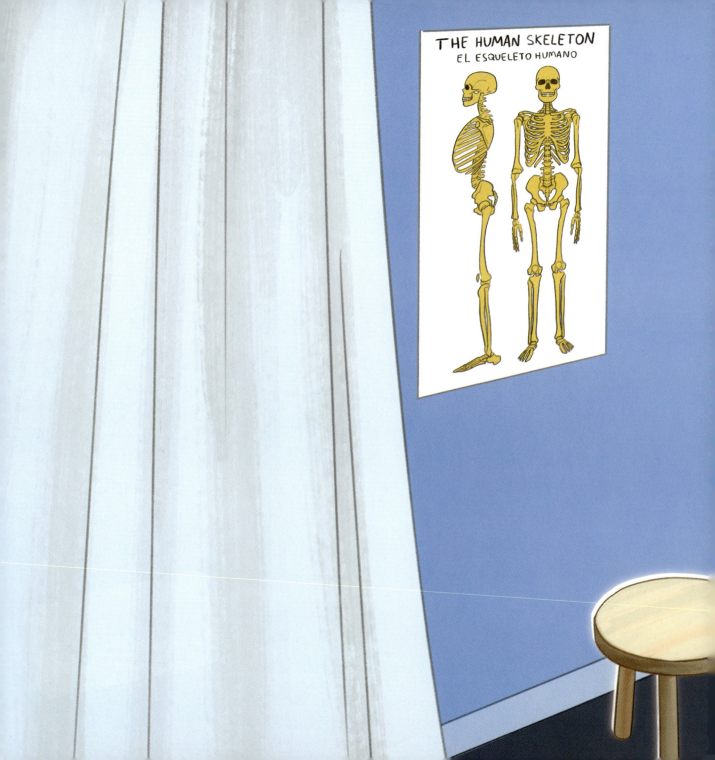

Why does my heart beat?

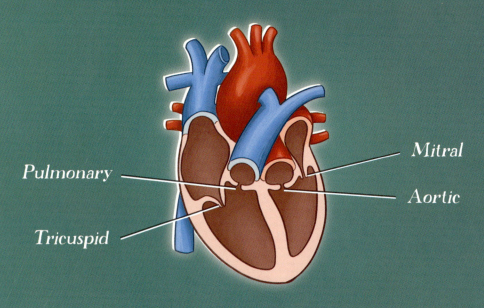

Heart Valves

Your heartbeat is the sound of your amazing heart pumping blood through your body. The valves inside your heart go *lub dub* as they open and close to let blood pass through.

Dr. Helen Taussig saw the connection between a healthy heart and a healthy patient. She worked with children whose hearts couldn't pump enough blood to their lungs.

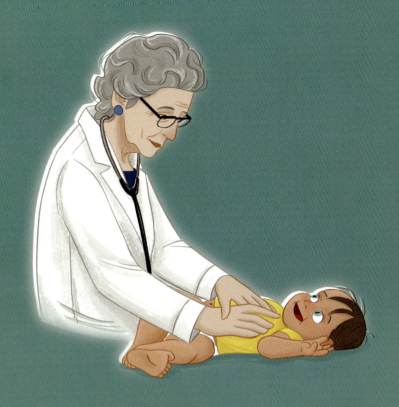

Nobody could figure out how to help, but Dr. Helen didn't give up. Even after she lost her hearing, she listened for that *lub dub* sound with her hands. Eventually, she found a way to solve the problem: a surgery that could create a new path, called a shunt, for blood to flow to the lungs.

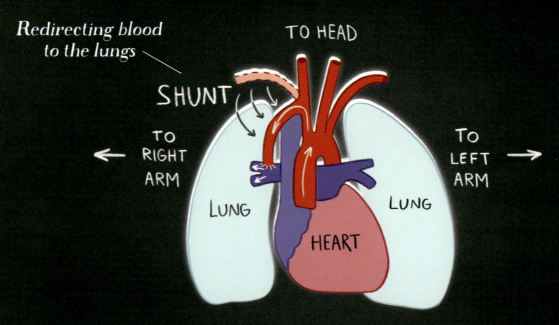

Blalock-Thomas-Taussig Shunt

When a surgeon finally agreed to try Dr. Helen's daring operation, it worked!

The Blalock-Thomas-Taussig shunt operation is still performed today, usually on babies who get to grow up thanks to Dr. Helen's efforts. Her revolutionary work made her the first doctor in the brand new healthcare specialty that she created: pediatric cardiology.

Dr. Helen Taussig
(HEL-ehn TAOW-sihg)
United States, 1898–1986

Who invented healthcare?

It's hard to say, because healthcare workers have been caring for people for as long as there have been people. Peseshet was in charge of women doctors in Egypt over 4,000 years ago. It was an important job, because just like today, people counted on doctors for their wisdom and healing expertise.

Peseshet and her doctors didn't have modern medicines or technology like ours, so they had to be very creative. Doctors of the time used fabric for bandages and made medicines with materials such as honey, coal, and plants. They set broken bones, healed wounds, and helped people with all kinds of health issues.

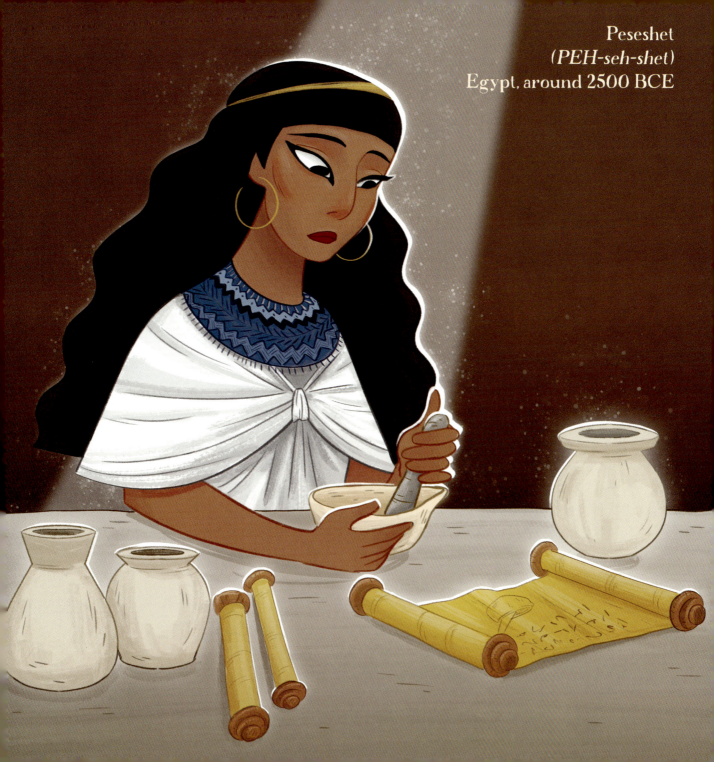

It's not just doctors who keep people healthy, though. There are many different healthcare workers who make a difference in our lives.

Like who?

Since ancient times, midwives like Xoquauhtli have cared for women and their unborn children. Xoquauhtli was a powerful member of the Aztec community. She visited pregnant women and kept track of their health. She encouraged the women to eat healthy foods so their babies could grow strong.

When it was time for a baby to be born, she used medicines to ease pain and quicken labor. After the baby arrived, Xoquauhtli cut the umbilical cord and made sure the baby stayed warm.

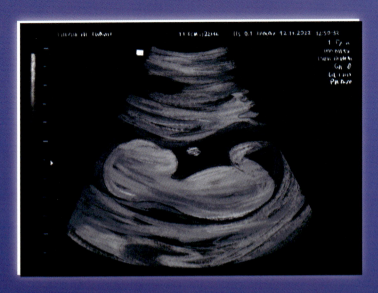

Ultrasound image of a fetus before birth

Midwives, nurses, and other healthcare workers today continue to do similar things. They also run tests and look at ultrasound pictures to watch developing babies as they grow. Soon after a baby is born, they are given a heel stick blood test.

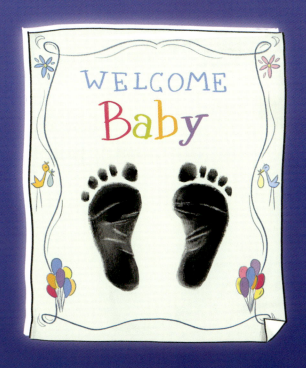

What's that?

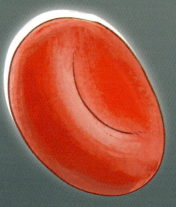

Sickle shape gets clogged in veins and doesn't do a good job of carrying oxygen

Regular red blood cell

Sickle cell

The heel stick blood test checks for conditions that need treatment right away, such as sickle cell disease. Dr. Angella Ferguson is the woman behind this test.

Sickle cell disease can change the shape of red blood cells and make a person very sick. Dr. Angella realized there wasn't enough information about sickle cell disease, especially in African American children. She researched the disease and taught other doctors how to diagnose and treat it.

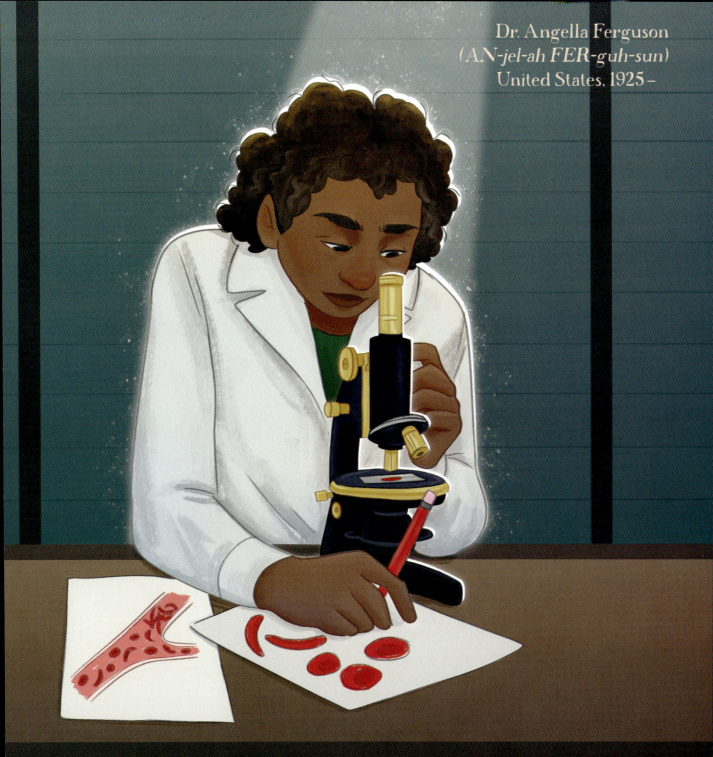

Dr. Angella Ferguson
(AN-jel-ah FER-guh-sun)
United States, 1925–

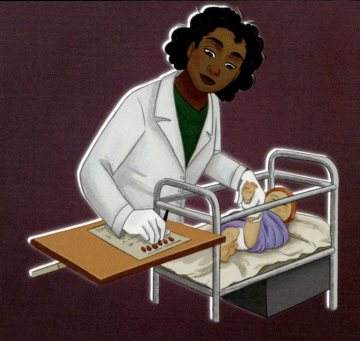

But sometimes people were sick for years before the disease was diagnosed. Dr. Angella kept working and created the world's first test for sickle cell disease.

At last, treatment could start at birth, immediately helping the 1,000 children worldwide who are born with the disease each day. Even though there is no cure, Dr. Angella's test and treatments help people with sickle cell disease live full lives.

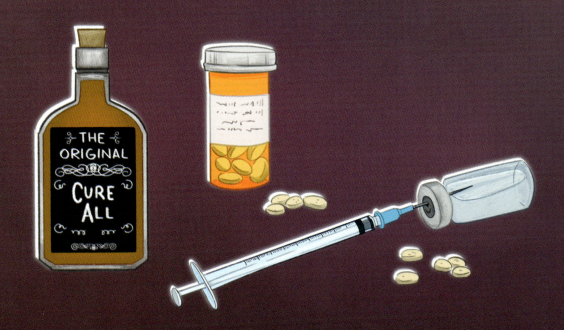

What is a cure?

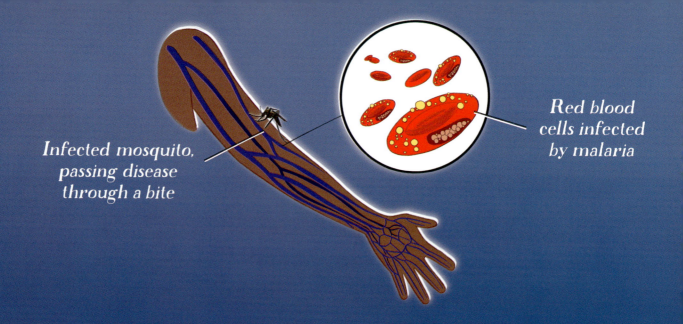

Infected mosquito, passing disease through a bite

Red blood cells infected by malaria

When a disease is cured, it means that treatment can make sick people healthy again. Researchers are working toward a cure for sickle cell and many other diseases.

Tu Youyou discovered a cure for a disease called malaria. She led a team that used pharmacology—the study of medicines and how they work in our bodies—to develop a new medicine.

Sweet Wormwood

Inventing a medicine takes lots of experimentation. Tu Youyou searched ancient Chinese medical texts looking for herbal recipes that might cure malaria. She discovered a plant extract called artemisinin after years of research and experiments.

Using creativity and simple equipment, she and her team used artemisinin to create a medicine to fight malaria. Tu Youyou volunteered as the first test subject. She was awarded a Nobel Prize for her world-changing work, and her medicine has saved over two hundred million lives.

Wow! What else have women discovered?

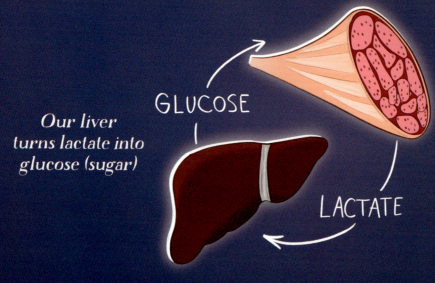

The Cori Cycle

Dr. Gerty Cori discovered the secret of how our bodies turn sugar into energy. She and her research partner created brand new ways to study the body and blood.

After six years of careful work, they figured out how our muscles and liver work together to use and store energy. The process became known as the Cori Cycle. The amazing discovery helped many people right away, especially those with diabetes.

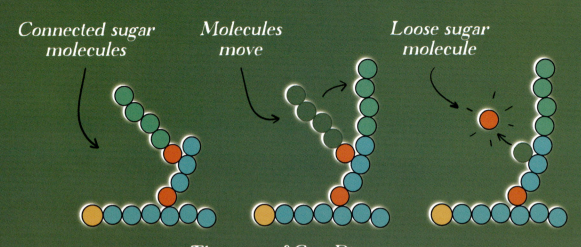

The cause of Cori Disease

Dr. Gerty was awarded a Nobel Prize for her groundbreaking work, but she wasn't done yet. She also discovered the cause of four types of energy-storage diseases. Sugars are stored in the body as molecules called glycogen. Glycogen acts like a fuel tank for our muscles. When our body can't store glycogen, it causes big health problems. Dr. Gerty's discoveries led to life-saving diagnoses and treatments.

Scientists worked in Dr. Gerty's laboratory to learn from her. Many of those scientists made important discoveries later on. Six of them won Nobel Prizes.

How can one person make such a big difference?

Some of the biggest improvements in medicine have happened because one person paid attention.

When Florence Nightingale first started her career as a nurse, she noticed that dirty conditions in hospitals seemed to be making patients worse. She began with simple steps like providing clean water and healthy food. She opened the windows for sunlight and fresh air. Patients began to improve more quickly.

Florence's Coxcomb Chart used to record patient data

Florence collected data that helped her point out problems with healthcare. Her work created new standards for cleanliness and safety in hospitals and doctors' offices, and improved the lives of many. However, Florence focused only on helping people who looked like her and shared her beliefs.

Even today, patients are not always treated equally. Modern healthcare workers are fighting to make sure every single person in need receives the best care possible. By paying attention to problems in the past and present, we can build a better future for all.

I want to help too!
What can I do?

Caring for others is a journey that can go many different ways. One of the first steps is taking care of yourself so you have the energy and ability to care for others. Healthcare workers also ask lots of questions and pay attention to how people are feeling.

Your journey might take you to places you'd never expect: to new discoveries, cures for illnesses, or even careers that haven't been invented yet!

But it can start with small actions, and by remembering that we are all connected. Curiosity and caring can change the world, one person at a time.

Glossary

BLALOCK-THOMAS-TAUSSIG SHUNT OPERATION: A surgical procedure used to increase blood flow to the lungs by bypassing the pulmonary artery when it is stuck shut (pulmonary stenosis).

CORI CYCLE: The process of the muscles and liver working together to use and store energy.

CURE: A medical treatment that can make a person healthy, including medicine, surgery, physical therapy, and more.

DIABETES: A condition in which the body doesn't produce enough insulin, doesn't produce any insulin, or struggles to use insulin. These problems change how the body turns sugar from food into energy.

DIAGNOSE: To find and categorize the reason a person feels unwell.

DOCTOR: A person who has trained for many years to check patients for health problems, make diagnoses, select the best treatments, and provide care.

FETUS: The unborn offspring of a human or other mammal that has been developing for more than eight weeks.

GLUCOSE: A natural sugar that is a source of energy for living things.

GLYCOGEN: The form in which bodies store glucose, mainly in the liver or muscles.

HEALTHCARE: Any jobs or services related to helping people feel well.

HEARTBEAT: The sound of heart valves opening and closing.

HEART VALVE: A structure in the heart that opens and closes to allow the blood to move in only one direction.

HEEL STICK BLOOD TEST: A blood test given to newborn babies, which involves pricking the heel of the foot to take a small blood sample. The sample is checked for conditions that need treatment right away, such as sickle cell disease. The test is also called the newborn screen or the state screen.

INSULIN: A hormone that regulates the amount of glucose in the blood.

LACTATE: A substance made by the muscles of the body as they turn sugar into energy.

MALARIA: A disease that affects blood cells, passed through the bite of infected mosquitoes.

MEDICINE: The field of science that deals with the prevention or cure of disease. This word also describes any substance that helps a person feel better.

MIDWIFE: A professional trained to assist women during pregnancy and childbirth.

PEDIATRIC CARDIOLOGY: A field of medicine that specializes in diagnosing and treating heart problems in children.

PHARMACOLOGY: The study of medicines and how they affect the body.

SICKLE CELL DISEASE: A disease that can change the shape of red blood cells or cause a shortage of red blood cells.

ULTRASOUND: The use of sound waves to produce pictures of the inside of the body.

UMBILICAL CORD: A natural tube that lets a developing baby receive nutrition from the mother's body before it is born. The cord must be cut after birth, and the spot where it was attached becomes the baby's belly button.

Science Wide Open: Women in Medicine
Copyright © 2022 Genius Games, LLC
Original series concept by John J. Coveyou

Written by Mary Wissinger
Illustrated by Danielle Pioli

Published by Science, Naturally!
English hardback first edition • September 2022 • ISBN: 978-1-938492-55-6
English paperback first edition • September 2022 • ISBN: 978-1-938492-56-3
English eBook first edition • September 2022 • ISBN: 978-1-938492-57-0

Spanish edition coming March 2023.

Enjoy all the titles in the series:
 Women in Biology • Las mujeres en la biología
 Women in Chemistry • Las mujeres en la química
 Women in Physics • Las mujeres en la física
 Women in Engineering • Las mujeres en la ingeniería
 Women in Medicine • Las mujeres en la medicina
 Women in Botany • Las mujeres en la botánica

Teacher's Guide available at the Educational Resources page of ScienceNaturally.com.

Published in the United States by:
 Science, Naturally!
   An imprint of Platypus Media, LLC
 750 First Street NE, Suite 700 • Washington, D.C. 20002
 202-465-4798 • Fax: 202-558-2132
 Info@ScienceNaturally.com • ScienceNaturally.com

Distributed to the trade by:
 National Book Network (North America)
   301-459-3366 • Toll-free: 800-462-6420
   CustomerCare@NBNbooks.com • NBNbooks.com
 NBN international (worldwide)
   NBNi.Cservs@IngramContent.com • Distribution.NBNi.co.uk

Library of Congress Control Number: 2022937701

10 9 8 7 6 5 4 3 2 1

The front cover may be reproduced freely, without modification, for review or non-commercial, educational purposes.

All rights reserved. No part of this publication may be reproduced or transmitted in any form or by any means, electronic or mechanical, including photography, recording, or any information storage and retrieval system, without permission in writing from the publisher. Front cover exempted (see above).

Printed in the United States of America.